Saint Joseph

Quiet Man of God

Mgr Seán Leonard, P.P.
&
Fr Edward Tuffy, P.P.

Messenger Publications,
37 Lower Leeson St.,
Dublin 2.

Published by
Messenger Publications,
37, Lower Leeson Street,
Dublin 2.
Tel: 676 7491. Fax: 661 1606.

With ecclesiastical permission,
Dublin 1997.

ISBN 1 872245 14 5

JOSEPH,

THE GREAT MAN OF GOD

by

**Mgr Seán Leonard, P.P.,
Swinford,
Co Mayo.**

The Real Joseph

I suppose this silent man of God, Joseph, must be the most maligned saint in heaven. There are so many things attributed to him, so many things he is supposed to have said and done, that he would hardly recognise himself. So without disfiguring him any further let us look at his life, insofar as it is recorded, and draw a few conclusions.

One of the things that has always intrigued me about Joseph is the way in which he is represented in Christian art. You will notice that he is very often portrayed as an old man, more like the father of our Lady than like her partner. Surely Joseph wasn't like that; surely the young Mary would never have settled for an old man as a partner.

I want to think of him as a young, manly person who was virtuous by effort rather than by age. I feel artists have done Joseph a great disservice by depicting him as a figure from whom the spark of life has been almost extinguished. One could hardly imagine the flight into Egypt taking place if Joseph were a pensioner!

The one fact about him that literally amazes me is the way in which he accepted the unique message Mary had one day to give him. Let's be realistic. Suppose a couple is engaged or recently married, and one day the lady says, 'By the way, I have a strange thing to tell you. I don't know if you will be able to accept this; I can only give you my word that it is true. I am expecting a baby and you are not the father and neither is any other man. The child I bear in my womb is miraculously fathered by God, and I must carry this blessing or cross until such time as what I am saying to you is revealed in some other way. I know you will find this hard to believe but I have nothing except my integrity to assure you'.

Now surely there is no man who would even listen to such a story, much less believe it; and this forces me to conclude that God played a special role in the life of Joseph, as he did in Mary's life. His acceptance of sheer faith carries a lesson to all of us Doubting Thomases, who are now at the stage where we will believe nothing unless we have empirical proof of its truth.

Perhaps this points to the reason why it is so difficult today to maintain Church membership. Failure to respond to faith is our great problem. The younger generation has the gift of being able to live with uncertainty more easily than older folk do. For them the loose ends are not always tied up, and any question about morality, and doubts about life and death and the hereafter, are all matters of personal opinion.

The Climate of the Times

There are so many voices crying out to be heard that people are in doubt as to who is the true and the false prophet. Today's people won't accept yesterday's solutions. If Joseph were around today, I fancy he would be invited to go on television and give his reasons for accepting this outlandish story from his partner, and I don't need to tell you how he would be treated when some of the high priests of television challenged his reasons. Interest from the media would be particularly keen, since the issue touches on sexuality, and Joseph would probably find himself - literally - speechless.

The climate of our times is hostile to faith; the sniper and the sceptic gain more recruits than the genuine enquirer. In that television discussion, we would hear opinions from all kinds of experts on how human life begins and how it doesn't. But it would ignore the fact that he who gave the first spark of life to the world, and did it without a partner, could again create the spark of life in the womb of an individual woman who had only to say, 'Let it happen to me as you have said' (Lk 1:38). I couldn't imagine Joseph, who said little in life, being a good television performer. His statements, based on sheer faith, would be treated in much the same way as many of the doctrines of the Church are treated today.

A Pearl of Great Price

I am a full-time parish priest stationed in the West of Ireland. When I was a young man I had a dream: I followed a star. It was to be a lifelong journey with nothing except my faith to guide me. Certainly, there were times when the light grew dim, but it never fully went out, and so I continued my journey until the star rested over the place where the child was.

I have stood by the bedside of many people about to die and have seen the wonder of their faith in St Joseph. I have seen St Joseph give countless happy deaths and have come away always strengthened in my belief. I cannot weigh or assess the value of that faith, nor can I in any way transmit it to others; I can only tell them about it.

The disappointing thing about having a Pearl of Great Price is that I get so little time to share it:

ten short minutes every Sunday morning. This is just one minuscule part of each parishioner's week and for all the rest of it there are so many influences working against me: the commercial world, the media, the entertainment element, the godless, the unbelieving, the unconvinced. I am not complaining. Our Lord hadn't even a microphone and he worked wonders. But then, of course, I'm not our Lord.

Try to visualise Joseph with his problem today. People with all the answers to everybody's problems would run to his assistance; one might come with referral literature; another might advise him to walk out on Mary and find some right woman who wouldn't drive him crazy and make him the laughing-stock of the country. But, you see, Joseph was wiser in his generation than the children of light. I believe that in the extraordinary circumstances of the birth of Christ there is a hidden message for all people of our day. It is very beautifully put in an American pro-life hymn:

God it is who gives all life, don't throw it away;
God it is who gives all breath, don't throw it away;
Listen, tender heart of gold, life in mother's womb
Laws must not destroy you, child; mother save your son.

God it is who gives all life; mother, love your child;
God it is who gives all breath; father, love your child;
Tiny feet and little hands, souls of precious life,
God's own gift of love to us; mother, save your child.

Now, the modern jargon and hypocritical cant, used to dress up murder in respectable clothing, is familiar to all of us: termination of pregnancy, the right to choose, 'my body is my own and I do with it as I please'. If Joseph took his lead from such slogans, we would have no Bethlehem, no Nazareth, no redemption and a poorer world. His good fortune in not having these catch-cries around in his day is surely a loud cry to our world. Every life is sacred and God has a plan for every person conceived, no matter what the tragic circumstances of that conception may have been. To try to thwart or frustrate that plan literally cries to heaven for vengeance.

Ordinary Saints

Most of the saints we know and pray to are all dressed-up people. Pictures of them give the impression of clean hands and gaudy clothes. St Patrick is a good example; even the way in which we pay tribute to him is on a grand scale. I've often thought that if somebody from outer space were to fly over Ireland on the seventeenth of March and guess what type of person was being honoured, his answer would be truly fascinating. Listening to all the bands he might feel we were paying tribute to some great musician; looking at the overflowing pubs that day he would certainly assume we must be paying tribute to the man who invented liquor; and listening to all the political speeches he would surely conclude that we were honouring some political figure. If this same alien looked down on Fifth Avenue in New York, as I did recently, he wouldn't know what to think. One thing I know: he would never guess that we were paying tribute to a saint, to our national apostle, so much have we commercialized our celebration.

And poor old St Joseph, whose feast comes two days later on the nineteenth of March, doesn't stand a chance after all the celebrations. It would be hard to make much of him anyway, with his old apron, his few crude tools, his head covered with sawdust, and with nothing to indicate his presence in the world except the sign hanging over the front door, *Joseph and Son Carpenters*.

We haven't given sufficient credit to the saints with welts on their hands, the ones who sweated and toiled to keep bread on the table, who never had their names in a book or hit the headlines in the newspapers. There are, I would hope and pray, more names of the Josephs of this world written in the book of life than Church history would indicate. I like to think that one of the first saints of the Church was an ordinary manual worker, and that the galleries of saints in heaven aren't full of nuns, popes, bishops and people who had public acclaim during their time on earth.

I've often attended a funeral of an old man or an old woman who was closer to God through goodness of life than many of those whose exclusive vocation it is to be holy. There wouldn't be twelve priests concelebrating the funeral Mass, and the area around the coffin wouldn't be like the Botanic Gardens. There would be very few Mass cards on the coffin. Still, I've often felt that the person being prayed for had retained the innocence of baptism and would easily settle into the exalted company of some of the glamorous saints we know so well.

I sometimes think of Joseph's funeral at times like that. The short ceremony over, I can imagine the mother and son walking quietly behind the coffin followed by a small crowd of villagers.

Nothing more. He was, after all, not a man of any great importance. The people on the way back home probably talked about him.

'A quiet man, very little to say, very good at his job, obliging too.' 'Great man for the synagogue on the Sabbath.' 'Never one to hit you too hard for the last shilling.' 'The son, of course, a peculiar man, is not a bit like the father. Very deep.' 'I hope he keeps on the business or we'll have nobody in the village to drive a nail for us.' 'I was there the night he died. He was sitting in the bed reciting psalms. The son and the mother joined in. Then his face changed. His head fell and that was it. I don't know what it did to me but I'll certainly never be the same again'.

Parents' Problems

In our day we hear quite a lot from parents about the problems of rearing teenagers, especially boys. Possibly you have had these problems yourself. You listen to all the experts in psychology, to teachers and priests and all those who you feel should know the answer; and really the answer comes best from yourself.

When there seems to be no answer to the situation, wouldn't it be wise to ask Joseph for help?

After all, he reared a teenager and would best understand what you're talking about. You see, there is some mysterious grace to be had from talking quietly to God and from praying to a saint about a particular difficulty. You will often find that in quiet moments of prayer, if you sit and listen, God will speak to you. Your mind becomes open to his voice and you come away more peaceful and better able to cope with what you originally thought was an impossible situation.

Vocations

I like to think about vocations as having started away back in the home in Nazareth, where Joseph and Mary ran the first major seminary and Jesus was the first student.

I can hear Joseph describing the situation. 'His mother was in charge of spiritual formation. She was good at that. I did the teaching. I taught him the psalms and all I knew about Scripture. He was a good student but I hadn't enough education to bring him very far. Anyway, he became a priest; in fact the supreme High Priest. He was the first priest of all time, and he led the way for all others. We had to teach him at home because we were very poor. We hadn't the money to send him to any of the big colleges in the city and there was no organization at that time to help parents in my predicament. So his mother and I did our best. It was hard at times but it was worth it.

'Of course our household seminary has been closed for nearly two thousand years but there are hundreds of others to cater for students all over the world. I still believe that every Christian home should be a miniature seminary where the seeds of vocation are sown. Mary and I will be present in such homes. We will be there to direct the work, for if we were not there the attempt would certainly fail.

'I hear of many twentieth century people in Western Europe complaining about lack of vocations and, at the same time, I hear of people in Poland and Korea and South America saying they can't cope with all who are applying. I recall the reverse situation two hundred years ago.

'Don't worry or fret over the ebb and flow of human history. Mary and her Son will look after that side of things and I'll tell them that you need vocations. They will listen to me, but I will need to be able to say that you asked me. You know that since I was a carpenter long ago I have never let down a customer. If I go to the Son for help, he won't refuse me because many times he came to me as a youngster and I never said no.'

The Priest in Every Parish

There is a man in every parish who, having no family, belongs to a family that is world-wide. He is called in as a witness and counsellor in all the most important affairs of civil life. No one comes into the world or goes hence without his concern. He receives the child from the arms of the mother and parts with it at the grave. He blesses and consecrates the cradle, the bridal chamber, the bed of death and the bier. He is the one whom innocent children learn to love, to venerate and to reverence. Even those who do not know him salute him as father.

At his side Christians lay bare the innermost thoughts of their souls, and weep their most sacred tears. He is one whose mission it is to console those who suffer the pains of body and soul. He is an intermediary between the affluent and the indigent. To his door will come alike the rich and the poor, the rich to give alms in secret and the poor to receive them without blushing. He belongs to no social class because he belongs equally to all.

He is one, in short, who is called to speak the truth unreservedly and whose speech, if it is to have the authority of his Lord and Master, must be rooted in faith and prayer and the integrity of his life.

Such is the priest, and no one has a greater opportunity for good when he fulfills his mission in life.

To give men of this calibre to the world is the concern of all people. We are to continue where Mary and Joseph left off. Our names are written in the book of life.

JOSEPH AND HIS FAMILY

by

**Fr Edward Tuffy, P.P.,
Bekan,
Claremorris,
Co Mayo.**

The Creation of the World

We read in Scripture (Gen 1:27) that 'God created man in the image of himself'. Surely being made in the image of God gives this new creature, man, the essence of immortality? Yet further on we read (Gen 2:7) that 'God shaped man from the soil of the ground'. Far from immortality, this seems to suggest thoughts of mortality, almost of finality. But the second part of that same verse gives us hope, because it tells us that 'God blew the breath of life into his nostrils, and man became a living being'. So we clearly have described in this passage a complex being, a being we call human. We are made in the image of God, having the gift of immortality, but we carry within ourselves the seeds of death.

Further on in that text (Gen 2:21-22) we are told that 'God made the man fall into a deep sleep. And, while he was asleep, he took one of his ribs ... and fashioned the rib ... into a woman'. The suggestion is unavoidable that there is some interdependence between man and woman.

Because of the disobedience of Adam and Eve, as related in the next chapter of Genesis, man's life was to become a struggle with the earth, with nature and even between man and man; but God promises a Redeemer and the victory of man over Satan: 'I shall put enmity between you and the woman,' God says to the serpent, 'and between your offspring and hers' (Gen 3:15).

In this victory, a woman was to play a very big part. From the time of Enoch, son of Seth, man called on God and looked forward to the coming of the Redeemer. So, through the books of the Old Testament, through the Patriarchs, Noah, Abraham, Isaac, Joseph and his brothers, through Moses and his people, through the Prophets, David and his people, we find people of faith. We also find a lack of faith and sinfulness.

I just mentioned the interdependence between woman and man. This interdependence is not only evident in the begetting of children, but it is also essential in their rearing. As we know from the Old Testament, it was then, as now, proper that parents remained together to rear their children and to be of help to one another.

The all-loving and all-wise God decreed from all eternity that not only would he create man in time with an intellect and free will, be they ever so finite, but that also in time he would stoop still further and that the Second Person of the Blessed Trinity would become man. This second union of

God with man by which God the Son took on our flesh is a mystery beyond our comprehension. It is a wonderful and beautiful story of God's loving desire to be in the hearts of mankind. In the words of Fulton Oursler, it is 'the greatest story every told'.

A Joyful Mystery

Let us for a moment pursue this extraordinary happening in time, recalling the great story as told to us by St Luke.

In the sixth month (I presume of Elizabeth's pregnancy) God sent the Angel Gabriel to a town in Galilee called Nazareth, to a virgin betrothed to a man named Joseph, who was a descendant of King David. The virgin's name was Mary. The angel greeted Mary with the words, 'Rejoice, you who are in God's favor! The Lord is with you' (Lk 1:28).

St Luke tells us that when Mary heard these words she was deeply troubled and began to reflect on this greeting, but the angel assured her there was no need to fear and went on to tell her that she was to become pregnant and give birth to a son whom she was to name Jesus.

This message caused turmoil in the mind of Mary because she was already betrothed to Joseph. It wrung from her this question, 'How can this come about since I have no knowledge of man?' (Lk 1:34). Her question indicated the nature of her relationship with Joseph and gives us the first insight into her own dispositions and the qualities of Joseph to whom she was betrothed.

The angel responds, 'The Holy Spirit will come upon you, and the power of the Most High will cover you with its shadow. And so the child will be holy and will be called Son of God' (Lk 1:35).

I am sure that Mary turned over this message in her mind because she spent much time in prayer and would have known the Scriptures. She would also have known that Christ was to be born of the tribe of Juda and of the house of David; and all were familiar with the prophecy of Isaiah, 'The Lord will give you a sign: It is this: the young woman is with child and will give birth to a son whom she will call Immanuel' (Is 7:14).

The angel also tells Mary that her aging cousin Elizabeth has conceived a son. After Mary received this message, St Luke tells us that she went with haste to visit her cousin Elizabeth.

One might validly ask why she did not tell her husband of the angel's message despite the urgency of her desire to be of assistance to her aging cousin. Might we even conjecture that despite her joy, which found its release in the Magnificat, she had an unease about Joseph's acceptance of her story?

Jewish Tradition

I would like to introduce here the marriage of Mary and Joseph. Fr Henry Gill S.J. in his book, *St Joseph,* tells us that in those days there were two stages in a Jewish marriage. First, the betrothal or espousal and, secondly, the reception of the bride into the home of her husband, which signified the consummation of their marriage.

The rite of betrothal or espousal consisted of an interchange of promises; also a sum of money was given by the bridegroom to the bride as a pledge of his fidelity. He also paid money to the bride's father in compensation for the loss she would be to the home. This rite was followed by a banquet which lasted for hours. It was at such a banquet in Cana of Galilee that Jesus, at his mother's request, performed his first miracle.

Although the newly espoused couple did not live together for some time, often for as long as a year, in practice their espousal had the force of a marriage *ratum sed non consummatum*. If the couple violated this custom and a child was conceived, it was looked on as legitimate. If the bride were unfaithful, she was liable to the same penalties as a woman guilty of adultery. So it seems to me that marriage took place at the espousal, and the fact that the couple did not live together was a respected custom.

At the time of the Annunciation, Mary and Joseph were espoused in the full Jewish fashion but had not come to live together. In their own hearts, as we learn from Mary's question to the angel, 'How can this come about since I have no knowledge of man?' (Lk 1:34), they had a marriage contract peculiar to themselves. It was in this period of time that God's intervention took place. Their espousal was unique, but their mission was also unique.

The man Joseph

St Joseph was destined to be the guardian and protector of the lives of Jesus and Mary in all the trials and difficulties of the Holy Family. He would be their support in their home at Bethlehem and in the foreign land of Egypt.

It was Joseph who snatched the child Jesus from the hands of Herod, and it was Joseph who was Mary's great comforter at the time the boy Jesus was lost in the temple. It was Joseph who by his trade earned a living for the Holy Family. It was from Joseph that the young man Jesus learned a trade. 'The carpenter's Son, as he was known, sanctified the home of Nazareth by prayer and word' (An tAth Conal Maclonrai).

It was the will of God that Joseph would appear before the world as the father of Christ and, in fact, from the outset Joseph did keep the notice of people from the mystery of the Virgin Conception and Birth until the fullness of time.

While it was the will of God that the Second Person of the Blessed Trinity would come amongst us and take flesh in the womb of one of our race, still it was proper that he would be born as the rest of us into a normal family background. It was right that, if Christ were to be born into the human family, in the eyes of the world he would have a human father. It was proper in the eyes of the world that, if Mary were to give birth to a son, she should have a husband.

Joseph learned that his spouse was pregnant. As he was a just and loving man, Joseph wished to save Mary from any embarrassment or punishment. Therefore his first inclination, we are told, was to divorce her informally. In other words, he would tell her it was all off and let her go her own way.

Let us think for a moment of his human feelings at a time like this. We can imagine the scar all this would leave on his life, the heartbreak, the babbling tongues, the hardship of coming to his decision. The unique marriage, based on such high ideals, was now the cause of much pain to him.

Mary must have worried too. Was she ever going to be understood? Was she ever going to be accepted? Was the very high ideal of the marriage covenant just to be a happy memory?

Divine Intervention

And then something happened to make Joseph change his mind. He received in a dream an angel's message about the divine intervention in his espousal with Mary. 'Joseph son of David, do not be afraid to take Mary home as your wife, because she has conceived what is in her by the Holy Spirit. She will give birth to a son and you must name him Jesus, because he is the one who is to save his people from their sins' (Mt 1:20-21). Joseph's role in

God's plan as the one committed with the care of his Son was explained to him. We are told that Joseph arose from his sleep and did as the angel told him. He immediately accepted that role.

Analysing this divine message to Joseph, Christ was to be born of David's royal blood and so he was, because Mary as well as Joseph was of the line of David. But here the angel seems to emphasise Joseph's descent from David. The angel also refers to Mary as Joseph's wife: 'Do not be afraid to take Mary home as your wife'. A wife is normally the mother of a man's children, but in this unique situation Joseph's wife Mary has conceived her baby of the Holy Spirit. So in this case the child to be born to Mary the wife of Joseph is, in the eyes of the world, his son. 'This is Joseph's son, surely?' they say in amazement at his preaching (Lk 4:23).

In the eyes of the law also, Jesus would be Joseph's son. We see this in the final part of the angel's message, 'You must name him Jesus'. In Jewish law it was the father's privilege and, indeed, his obligation to name his child. We must, however, remember that the position in which Joseph now finds himself arises because he is the husband of Mary.

A Kind Protector

Joseph assumes the role as head of the little home at Nazareth. It was as head of the home that he took Mary to Bethlehem for the census because he belonged to the line of David, and Bethlehem was the town of David. By journeying to Bethlehem, Joseph could insert the name, 'Jesus, son of Joseph of Nazareth', in the registry of the Roman Empire. We remember the hardships which the young mother and her husband endured on that occasion. We can easily imagine the anxiety of the young man Joseph as he went from inn to inn, finding there was no room for them anywhere. Eventually they took shelter in a cave used for animals and it was here that the baby was born.

Joseph, the legal father, with Mary his wife, took the child to the Temple to present him to the Lord. There he offered a pair of pigeons, the offering which the very poorest were obliged to make.

Joseph worked hard in Bethlehem to provide food and accommodation. He had only partly achieved this when Herod ordered all male children of two years of age and under in his kingdom to be put to death, thinking that Jesus would not escape his net; but again Joseph was warned in a dream to take Mary his wife and the child and go to Egypt.

So Joseph got up and told Mary, and together they packed some food and necessities for the journey. I am sure they packed some tools so that in a foreign land he would earn enough to keep Mary and the child. Already, no doubt, Jesus was beginning to perceive the love of a good and gentle mother, and the security of a kind and diligent father.

During their sojourn in Egypt, where Jews were not welcome, the boy would experience more and more the hard work of Joseph, and would perceive his diligence and commitment to his family and to his Creator. Jesus would realise by his human instincts that the man appearing before humanity as his father was indeed, like his mother, chosen by God.

After Herod's death, we find Joseph using his own prudence for the safety of the child Jesus. They did not return to Bethlehem because Herod's son Archelaus ruled in place of his father. Joseph must have known enough about him not to trust him, so instead he took the family to Nazareth. In doing so, he was fulfilling a prophesy: that Christ would be called a Nazarene.

'My Father's House'

We hear no more of the Holy Family until Christ is twelve years old. The intervening time is spent, I presume, in happiness. But such happy days did not continue even for the Holy Family and so we find Joseph and Mary in sorrow in the Temple in Jerusalem. They had gone there with the boy to celebrate the Feast of the Passover. They were Jews and people of prayer, and so they kept the great feast, the commemoration of their deliverance from Egypt. After the festival was over they returned home, each thinking that the boy Jesus was with the other, only to discover after a day's journey that their child was lost.

They returned to Jerusalem to look for him and after three days of great anxiety they found him in the temple talking to the doctors of the law whom he astonished with his wisdom and answers. It was Mary who spoke to him, 'My child, why have you done this to us? See how worried your father and I have been, looking for you'(Lk 2:48). Mary emphasises Joseph's great fatherly love and anxiety. Christ's reply to her emphasises his obligations to his father in heaven. 'Did you not know that I must be in my Father's house? (Lk 2:49).

Nevertheless, in obedience to them he went down with them to Nazareth and was dutiful to them. It is worth noting at this stage that we do not find in the Scriptures any spoken word of Joseph. His mission was one of prayer, love and work.

All we know of the next eighteen years is that Jesus grew in wisdom and grace before God and man. Perhaps he learned the carpenter's trade from Joseph and helped contribute to the home. It would appear that Joseph died during this time.

A Father's Love

In conclusion, I want to introduce a very personal thought. I was away from home when my father died and it was late at night when I returned. His body was laid out on the bed, and as I stood and looked at his hands, now clutching a crucifix and his rosary beads, I thought of how hard those hands had worked for me.

I thought of how often he had denied himself that I might have. I thought of all I had learned from him. It was then, when I could act the man no longer and tears began to run down my face, that my mother who was standing beside me put her arm over my shoulder. I realised then that they were two, that it was in the unity and trust of the two that I was loved and that it was by their example above all else that I was taught.

I do not want to sound presumptuous, but I would love to think that Jesus felt as I did, standing beside Mary and looking at the dead Joseph - Joseph who was everything to him that a most diligent and loving father could be.

PRAYER TO ST JOSEPH FOR VOCATIONS

O Jesus,
send labourers into your field,
which are awaiting
holy apostles, saintly priests,
heroic missionaries,
gentle and tireless sisters
and dedicated brothers.
Enkindle in the hearts
of young men and women
the spark of a vocation.
Grant that Christian families
may desire to give to your Church
helpers in the work of tomorrow.

Based on a prayer of Pope John XXIII